WORLD LEADERS

STEWART ROSS

Wayland

WORLD LEADERS

Titles in this series:

Propaganda
Victims of War
Women's War
World Leaders

Cover illustration: A 1939 poster showing Hitler and Stalin, soon to be on opposite sides, jogging along in an uneasy alliance.

First published in 1993 by
Wayland (Publishers) Limited
61 Western Road, Hove
East Sussex BN3 1JD, England

© Copyright 1993 Wayland (Publishers) Limited

Series editor: Paul Mason
Designers: Malcolm Walker/John Yates

British Library Cataloguing in Publication Data
   Ross, Stewart
   World Leaders. – (Era of the Second World
   War Series)
   I. Title II. Series
   940.53

ISBN 0-7502-0776-0

Typeset in the UK by Dorchester Typesetting Group Ltd
Printed and bound in Italy by Rotolito Lombarda S.p.A.

Picture acknowledgements
The publishers would like to thank the following for permission to use their photographs in this book: Arkiv fur Kunst und Geschichte/Image Select *cover*, 13, 23; Camera Press 8, 10, 20, 30, 31; Imperial War Museum 4, 11, 12, 14 bottom, 18, 21, 22, 27, 28, 29, 32, 34, 37, 40, 41; Popperfoto 9, 16, 19, 42; Topham/Associated Press 6, 14 top, 35, 36, 38, 39; Wayland Picture Library 5, 7, 43.

Contents

Dictators and democrats

The era of the Second World War threw up a number of remarkable war leaders. Some, such as Germany's Adolf Hitler and the USSR's Joseph Stalin, were dictators who appeared to exercise almost complete personal control over their countries. Other leaders, including Britain's Winston Churchill and President Franklin Roosevelt of the USA, headed democratic states. They too were very powerful, with far more authority than they would have had in peace time.

The Second World War can be seen as a struggle

The Allies' three most important leaders: (left to right) Joseph Stalin of the USSR, Franklin Roosevelt of the USA and Winston Churchill of Britain meeting in Tehran, 1943.

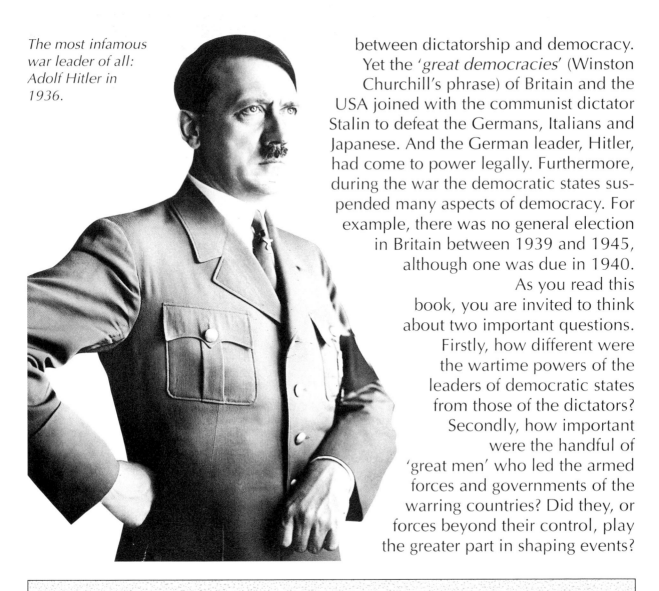

The most infamous war leader of all: Adolf Hitler in 1936.

between dictatorship and democracy. Yet the '*great democracies*' (Winston Churchill's phrase) of Britain and the USA joined with the communist dictator Stalin to defeat the Germans, Italians and Japanese. And the German leader, Hitler, had come to power legally. Furthermore, during the war the democratic states suspended many aspects of democracy. For example, there was no general election in Britain between 1939 and 1945, although one was due in 1940.

As you read this book, you are invited to think about two important questions. Firstly, how different were the wartime powers of the leaders of democratic states from those of the dictators? Secondly, how important were the handful of 'great men' who led the armed forces and governments of the warring countries? Did they, or forces beyond their control, play the greater part in shaping events?

The historian A J P Taylor was quite sure how important the major war leaders were: '*Essentially only the political leaders counted. It is hardly an exaggeration to say that four men – Hitler, Churchill, Roosevelt and Stalin – made every important decision of the war personally.*' (*The Second World War.*)

Other historians are less sure of the importance of individuals. They have suggested that without the backing of other powerful forces, leaders could not have had as much influence as they did. Hitler, for example, was backed in his bid for power in Germany by a powerful and wealthy group of industrialists, without whom he could not have become German leader.

Adolf Hitler
(1889–1945)

> 'We are all convinced . . . that he [Hitler] is the mouthpiece and pathbreaker of the future. Therefore we believe in him. Beyond his human form, we can see . . . the active grace of destiny.' (Joseph Goebbels, *Diary*.)
>
> 'Pastor Dietrich Bonhoffer, a descendant of eminent Protestant clergymen on both sides of his family . . . regarded Hitler as Antichrist and . . . believed it a Christian duty to eliminate him.' (William L Shirer, *The Rise and Fall of the Third Reich*.)

Probably no man this century aroused such strong emotions in people as Adolf Hitler. No world leader was so fascinating or was believed to have had so much influence on events. His controversial personality dominated the era of the Second World War.

Born in Austria, Hitler fought for Germany in the First World War. Like many Germans, in 1918 he felt bitter that the German armies had surrendered without being defeated. He believed they had been '*stabbed in the back*' by the politicians.

After the war Hitler became a politician. He was an energetic member of the extreme right wing National Socialist (Nazi) party. During the 1920s the Nazis made little headway. But the world economic crisis which began in 1929 brought severe hardship to millions of Germans, persuading many of them to look to the Nazis for salvation. Hitler shared the rising discontent with the Weimar Republic (see panel) and understood the popular desire for law and order. In the March 1932 presidential elections he received 30 per cent of the votes. Four months later the Nazis were the largest single party in the *Reichstag* (German parliament), although they did not have an overall majority. On 30 January 1933 Hitler was made chancellor of Germany by the President.

German troops surrendering in the First World War. Hitler carefully exploited the humiliation felt by many Germans at the surrender of their undefeated armies in 1918.

Germany's crisis
Germany faced a double crisis in the early 1930s.
1 The Weimar Republic, the political system set up after Germany's defeat in the First World War, was unable to provide stable government.
2 Much of Germany's recovery after the war depended on money borrowed from the USA. After the 1929 Wall Street Crash many US financiers demanded their money back, bankrupting German businesses and causing high unemployment (1928 1 million unemployed; 1933 over 6 million).
  Hitler's Nazis announced that they were the last hope for a desperate people.

Hitler speaking at a public meeting. In the 1930s his brilliant speeches at huge, carefully-managed rallies attracted many Germans to the Nazi cause.

Hitler was a brilliant and ruthless politician. Once the Nazis were in power, they were determined never to give it up. Guided by Hitler, they forced through an Enabling Law (March 1933), which gave Hitler special authority to deal with Germany's crisis. By 1936 most opposition had been eliminated, the Nazis had seized control of the army and declared Hitler '*Führer* [leader] *of the German Reich*'. The Nazi government began spending millions of marks on re-armaments and public works, such as the famous autobahn motorways, and the economy started to recover. Hitler's declared aim, set out in his book *Mein Kampf* [My Struggle], was to make the Germans the '*master race*' of Europe.

The 1919 Treaty of Versailles, drawn up after the First World War, imposed very harsh terms on Germany. As well as having to pay heavy reparations, it lost much territory inhabited by German-speaking peoples. Hitler made no secret of the fact that he wanted to take this land back. On 7 March 1936, Hitler sent German troops into the demilitarized zone of the Rhineland. Although ordered to return if they were opposed, the troops met with no resistance. Two years later, having come to agreements with the Japanese and Italians, Hitler again ignored the Treaty of Versailles by uniting Germany and Austria.

In September 1938 Hitler prepared to invade Sudetenland in western Czechoslovakia, which had a large German population. A European war seemed imminent. But at a meeting at Munich on 29 September Hitler persuaded the British and French Prime Ministers, Chamberlain and Daladier, that Sudetenland was his '*last territorial ambition*', and he was allowed to go ahead with his occupation. After the occupation of the rest of Czechoslovakia in March 1939, Britain guaranteed the independence of Hitler's next target, Poland. Having negotiated a non-aggression pact with the USSR on 23 August, on 1 September 1939 Hitler's forces invaded Poland. Britain and France declared war on Germany two days later.

German light tanks entering Poland, September 1939. Britain and France had said that they would not allow Poland to be invaded: when Hitler ordered his troops to invade, Britain and France declared war on Germany.

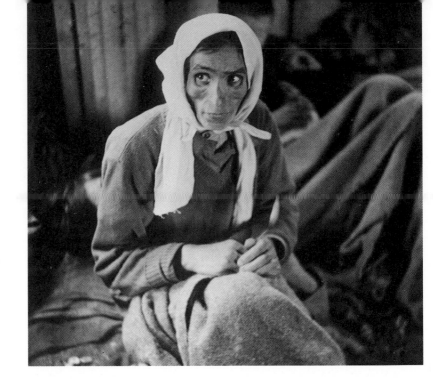

A starving female inmate of a Nazi concentration camp. Why do you think Hitler carefully made sure he was not directly associated with such atrocities?

Did Hitler want war?
Some scholars believe that Hitler's foreign policy risked war, but did not plan for it. They say that *Mein Kampf* was propaganda, and that he advanced step by step, deciding on his next move, only when he saw how things stood. They argue that, after what he had seen at Munich, he thought that Britain and France would not intervene when he invaded Poland. Other experts say that all along Hitler followed the aggressive foreign policy he had sketched out in *Mein Kampf*, knowing it was bound to lead to war.

In 1938 Hitler had removed the German army commanders who disagreed with his policies. After the outbreak of war he devoted himself to military matters, taking complete command on 19 December 1941. This meant that individuals within the Third Reich such as Himmler (police chief and minister of the interior) and Air Force Commander Goering were able to build up huge personal power.

The most dreadful aspect of Nazi government was the persecution of the Jews, which in 1941 became an attempt to wipe them out completely. Hitler had fed German anti-Semitism, issued anti-Jewish laws and helped establish concentration camps. He certainly knew and approved of the terrible sufferings of the Jewish people. Perhaps fearing for his reputation, Hitler left the detailed arrangements of the concentration camps to others.

Hitler's ability as a military commander is uncertain. He supported the successful tactics of *Blitzkrieg* (lightning war) – a term he first used at a Nazi rally in 1935 – which allowed his armies to sweep across Western Europe in 1940. On 22 June 1941, Hitler's forces made a surprise attack on the USSR. At first the armies made rapid progress, but by the winter their advance had been halted by a Soviet counter-attack. Hitler's decision not to allow a German retreat at this point may have saved his armies from destruction by the advancing Soviets. Throughout the war his leadership is believed to have inspired German troops to remarkable acts of bravery: General Rommel noted that, '*At the Führer's command they were ready to sacrifice themselves to the last man.*' It was partly to prevent this happening that Rommel joined a plot to assassinate Hitler in July 1944.

On the other hand, Hitler rarely visited the battle fronts, leaving him out of touch with military reality. In May 1940, when the Allied armies were at his mercy, for some reason he did not order his tank divisions to move in for the kill. This allowed the bulk of the British Army to flounder home from Dunkirk. Later, particularly in North Africa, Italy and the USSR, Hitler's

On 29 April 1945 Hitler married his female companion Eva Braun. Before they committed suicide the next day, Hitler defended his career in a *Political Testament*:
'I have been actuated solely by love and loyalty to my people . . . It is untrue that I, or anyone else in Germany, wanted the war in 1939 . . . I die with a happy heart, aware of the immeasurable deeds of our soldiers at the front . . . That from the bottom of my heart I express my thanks to you all is just as self-evident as my wish that you should . . . on no account give up the struggle . . . against the enemies of the Fatherland.'

Uneasy friendship: Hitler greets Erwin Rommel, the brilliant general who finally joined a plot to assassinate him in 1944.

refusal to allow his forces to withdraw tied the hands of the field commanders and led to pointless loss of life. His 1944 Ardennes offensive (the Battle of the Bulge) was costly and stood little chance of success, and his decision never to surrender led to ghastly slaughter and destruction in Germany during 1945.

Since 1945 millions of words have been written about Hitler. Some accounts emphasize his abilities, others play them down, saying that he rose to power on a wave of German discontent as the political spokesman of German industrialists. Hitler has been criticized as a bungler who, had he listened to sensible advice, might have made his dreams of a 'Thousand-Year Reich' come true. Others believe that it was not his talents which enabled him to achieve so much, but the feebleness of those who opposed him, both within Germany and in other countries.

Had he lived in a different country during a different age, Hitler might have achieved nothing. But he was born into circumstances which allowed his ideas to spread and his policies to be carried out.

A man in a million? A famous 1914 photograph of the declaration of the First World War shows the young Hitler as just one of a huge crowd.

Benito Mussolini (1883–1945)

Mussolini was the first fascist dictator to come to power. He was also the least tyrannical and in the end the most ridiculous. Invited by the King of Italy to become prime minister in 1922, he gradually set up a one-party state. By 1929 his Fascist Council had replaced the cabinet and from then until 1943 Mussolini was the supreme authority in Italian politics. His government emphasized obedience to the leader, public works, pride in the Italian state and the virtues of war. The regime was supported by brilliant propaganda campaigns, which built up a heroic image of the country's *Duce* (leader).

Mussolini believed in war as a way of uniting people and bringing glory to the Italian state. '*Fascism*', he said in 1932, '*believes neither in the possibility nor the utility* [usefulness] *of perpetual peace.*' This attitude was

Mussolini's fascism

The *Fascist Programme* of 1922 was typical of Mussolini's vague, emotional appeals to all groups of people: '*Fascists, Italians! The hour of the decisive battle has struck . . . Fascism* [does not] *march against the members of the public administration, but against a class of imbecile and weak-minded politicians . . . The* [middle class] *knows that fascism wishes to give aid to all those forces which advance its economic expansion and well-being. The working class . . . have nothing to fear from fascism. Their just rights will be loyally preserved . . . We call upon Almighty God . . . to witness that only one impulse moves us, only one desire unites us: to contribute to the salvation and to the greatness of our country.*'

Fascist propaganda shows Mussolini's face imprinted on the map of Rome. The message: Mussolini represents the whole of Italy and its capital, Rome.

all very well when Mussolini bullied weaker states. But unsuccessful involvement in the Second World War brought the fascist regime down and led to his death.

Involvement in the Second World War was Mussolini's fatal mistake. The war ruined Italy's economy and, partly as a result, was not popular at home. The Italian army and navy were heavily defeated. To make matters worse, the dictator declared war on the USA, sent troops to help Hitler in the USSR, and issued a string of unrealistic commands that his generals could not obey. By the end of 1941 Italy was almost entirely dependent on German military and economic aid.

Mussolini's health began to give way and he grew increasingly pessimistic about the chances of victory. The Allies invaded Sicily on 10 July 1943. A fortnight later *Il Duce* was forced to resign. Rescued from prison by a daring German raid in September, he headed a fascist regime in Northern Italy until April 1945, when he was captured and executed by his own countrymen.

Over the years Mussolini came to believe much of the exaggerated praise heaped upon him in fascist propaganda. Overshadowed by Hitler and always promising more than he could deliver, by 1940 Mussolini had become little but a 'ludicrous legend'. When he died five years later he was no longer a leader of any importance on the world scene.

After execution, the bodies of Mussolini, his mistress Clara Petacci and other prominent fascists were strung up by their feet in a gruesome gesture of humiliation.

Francisco Franco (1892–1975)

Franco spent his early life as a soldier in the Spanish army. Having distinguished himself fighting in Morocco, then a Spanish colony, in 1934 he became involved in politics when he broke up a group of communist miners in Spain. By 1936 Franco was chief of the general army staff and in position to play a key role in Spain's future.

Spain, which had become a republic in 1931, was a bitterly divided country. There were right-wing groups, such as the church, the army, wealthy landowners, monarchists and the Spanish fascist party (*Falange*). Ranged against them, but suspicious of each other, were the numerous reforming and left-wing groups of the Popular Front. These included liberals, socialists, communists and anarchists. The situation was further complicated by Basque and Catalan separatists from the north of the country, who wished to break away from Spain.

In February 1936 the Popular Front won the elections and formed a government. Alarmed by the success of the left and mounting violence, on 18 July Franco decided to move. He led an army revolt in Morocco and crossed to the mainland, appealing to all right-wing groups: '*Spaniards! To whoever feels a holy love of Spain . . . to those who have sworn to defend Spain from her enemies, the nation calls you to her defence. Are we to abandon Spain to her enemies? . . . No!*' Spain was plunged into years of civil war. Three months later the military named Franco as head of the Nationalist state.

A 1937 Spanish postcard illustration linking Franco with Hitler and Mussolini. During the Spanish Civil War Franco was happy to accept the support of fascists at home and abroad.

¡HEIL HITLER!

¡VIVA ESPAÑA!

¡VIVA L'ITALIA!

Franco (centre) attending a funeral at the height of the Spanish Civil War (1937), which his action had begun the previous year. When the Second World War broke out in 1939, he refused to become actively involved.

The Spanish Civil War, July 1936–April 1939

In some ways the war was a dress rehearsal for the Second World War. Franco led a right-wing Nationalist coalition against a loose union of Republicans. The Nationalists eventually won because they were better led and armed, and because they received important support from Hitler and Mussolini. Almost 1 million people died in the conflict.

1936 Nationalists move to the mainland. With German and Italian assistance, by the end of the year Franco controls half of Spain. The Republicans are helped by the USSR and International Brigades of volunteers.

1937 Franco fails to take the centre of Spain but defeats the Basques in the north-west. German air power used to devastating effect, notably on the town of Guernica.

1938 Republican-held area cut in two and their offensive defeated.

1939 Franco takes Barcelona and Madrid. War ends.

After the Civil War the Nationalist government of Franco, *el Caudillo* (the leader), was recognized by the major democratic powers. He strengthened his position by building up the *Falange Tradicionalista*, the only party allowed in Spain, and organizing the country along the lines of Mussolini's Italy. Franco knew that the Spanish were tired of war, and he refused to be drawn into the Axis alliance. On 23 October 1940 he met Hitler at Hendaye in France to discuss a possible alliance. To Hitler's frustration, Franco proved one of the few world leaders whom he could not overawe and Spain remained neutral. In deciding on neutrality, had Franco decided to reject Hitler's fascism? Or was the policy the only realistic one for a nation too divided and exhausted by years of civil war to fight any more?

After the war, despite condemnation by the victorious Allies, Franco held his independent line. In 1947 he declared that he would remain *el Caudillo* for life. However, as he grew older he gradually made his regime more liberal, eventually handing over power two years before his death.

Neville Chamberlain (1869–1940)

British Prime Minister Neville Chamberlain has often been blamed, perhaps unfairly, for a tragic lack of political judgement. Of all the anti-fascist leaders in power during the 1930s, he has been most strongly criticized for not taking a strong stand against the ambitions of Nazi Germany. Yet he belonged to a generation which had witnessed the slaughter of millions of young men in the First World War and for whom another war was almost unthinkable. At least until 1939 Chamberlain was not out of touch with popular opinion – he represented it.

Chamberlain became prime minister of Britain's National Government on 28 May 1937. He had proved a conscientious and hard-working politician. But he lacked experience in foreign affairs, which made it difficult for him to handle the tricky international situation. Until March 1939, when Hitler occupied the Czechoslovakian capital of Prague, Chamberlain followed a policy of appeasement (see box on the next page). He did not act when Hitler

Appeasement

The policy Chamberlain's policy of appeasement, which had widespread support in Britain until 1939, meant avoiding war by talking with Hitler face-to-face and giving way to his demands.

The defence • Remembering the horrors of 1914-18, almost anything was better than another large war. • Communism, which promised world-wide revolution, was more to be feared than the Nazis – a strong Germany would act as a buffer against the communist USSR. • Until 1939, the British people would not have supported another European war. • Protected by the Royal Navy and the Maginot Line, Britain and France were safe from a Nazi attack. • The longer war was delayed the better, as Britain needed time to re-arm. • Germany had been harshly treated by the 1919 Treaty of Versailles – Hitler's aggression was therefore understandable and, to some extent, justifiable.

The criticism • Appeasement confirmed Britain's weakness and so encouraged Hitler to make more and more demands. • Chamberlain paid more attention to his personal advisers than to the warnings of the Foreign Office. • Britain had a duty to support the small democracies of Eastern Europe.

broke the Treaty of Versailles and united Germany with Austria in 1938.

Later in the same year Chamberlain gave way to Hitler's demands for the Sudetenland in Czechoslovakia and returned home to announce, '*I believe it is peace for our time.*' After meeting Hitler at Munich he said of the fascist dictator, '*I got the impression that here was a man who could be relied upon when he had given his word.*' History proved Chamberlain wrong.

When he saw how he had been mistaken, the prime minister guaranteed Poland's independence and finally went to war when Hitler invaded that country on 1 September 1939. But even at this late stage Chamberlain had tried to get the Poles to give way to Hitler's demands, and his unsuccessful efforts to ally with the USSR were at best half-hearted.

Ill and depressed, Chamberlain resigned as prime minister on 10 May 1940. He remained in the government until his death in November.

Dead soldiers of the First World War. Politicians such as Chamberlain remembered the numbers that had died, and preferred almost anything to another war.

Winston Churchill (1874–1965)

When Britain went to war in 1939 Winston Churchill was sixty-five years old. He had been a soldier, journalist, writer and politician, but he had not held government office since 1929. Many thought his career was over.

During the 1930s Churchill had campaigned on two issues. One was his determination to preserve the British Empire in the face of calls for independence. The other was his unfashionable opposition to the fascist dictators and his demands for British re-armament. In recognition of this, on the out-break of war Prime Minister Chamberlain appointed him First Lord of the Admiralty, a post he had held from 1911 to 1915.

On 10 May 1940, as (in Churchill's words) an *'avalanche of fire and steel'* rolled westwards towards the Channel, Chamberlain resigned. Senior politicians

---

Churchill and Appeasement

Churchill was one of the few British politicians who resolutely opposed Chamberlain's policy of appeasing Hitler and Mussolini. At the time his speeches seemed narrow-minded, especially to those who saw communism as a greater threat:

1934 *'I dread the day when the means of threatening the heart of the British Empire should pass into the hands of the present rulers of Germany . . . I dread that day, but it is not perhaps far distant.'*

1938 The Munich agreement was, *'only the first sip, the first foretaste of a bitter cup which will be proffered to us year by year, unless . . . we arise again and take our stand for freedom as in the olden times.'*

Churchill at a weapons test in 1940. Pictures such as this were used to portray Churchill as a determined fighter who would never give in to his enemies.

agreed that Churchill's hour had come, and he was made prime minister.

Churchill's coalition government lasted until July 1945. As prime minister and minister of defence, Churchill had many powers. The War Cabinet gave him control over every detail of the war effort. Even the men commanding the armed forces, the chiefs of staff, generally went along with his ideas. He summed up his powers thus: '*All I wanted was compliance with my wishes after discussion.*' On occasion Churchill faced opposition in parliament, most notably in July 1942 when the Germans sank 21 of the 34 ships on a convoy to the USSR. Nevertheless, his position was never seriously threatened; the British people were unable to vote for or against his government in an election until 1945, although one should have been held in 1940. In the influence he wielded and the way in which the media built up an image of him as an infallible chief, Churchill was not unlike the totalitarian leaders. Rarely in modern British history had so much power been

Churchill's oratory
In the end Churchill's reputation rested to a great extent on his ability to capture – and even mould – the mood of the British people. Never was this more plain than in his speeches of 1940. On 13 May, in an effort to prepare the British people for the hardships ahead, he told the House of Commons: '*I would say to the House . . . . I have nothing to offer but blood, toil, tears and sweat . . . you ask, What is our aim? I can answer in one word: Victory – victory at all costs, victory in spite of all terror, victory however long and hard the road may be; for without victory there is no survival.*'

Churchill just before broadcasting the news that Hitler's Germany had been defeated, in May 1945. Five years before, his brilliant radio speeches had been the single most important factor in convincing Britain that defeat was not inevitable.

On 18 June, in what was probably his most famous speech, he was most concerned with raising morale: *'I expect that the Battle of Britain is about to begin. Upon this battle depends the survival of Christian civilization . . . if we fail, then the whole world . . . will sink into the abyss of a new Dark Age. Let us therefore brace ourselves to our duties, and so bear ourselves that, if the British Empire and its Commonwealth last for a thousand years, men will say "This was their finest hour".'*

One German general reckoned Churchill's leadership was worth thirty armoured divisions.

concentrated in the hands of one person.

Although no one denies Churchill's remarkable contribution to his country's war effort, he did make strategic misjudgements. He may have overestimated the ability of massive bombing raids to damage Germany's industrial production in 1942-3. His insistence on sending convoys to Russia, many of which sustained very heavy losses, wasted precious resources. And his belief, shared by many others, that Japan would not be drawn into the war meant that Britain was ill prepared for a land war in the Far East.

On the other hand, Churchill understood that Britain could not possibly win the war alone. He surprised many people in the way he warmly accepted the Soviet Union as an ally after Hitler attacked it in June 1941. Churchill worked even harder for US support. Many of his speeches were aimed at US audiences as well as British. He enjoyed a close friendship with President Roosevelt, whose country remained neutral until December 1941. The relationship resulted in the US

Churchill the actor. Like many war leaders, Churchill had a strong sense of theatre and loved showing off before crowds. He made his bowed stance, cigar and two-fingered victory sign symbols of his country's will to fight.

The 1945 General Election

Labour	393 seats
Conservative	213
Liberals	12
Independent	22

To many observers the defeat of Churchill's Conservative Party was a shock. But the British people had had enough of foreign affairs and felt that Labour offered better prospects for post-war social and economic recovery. Churchill was understandably upset by their decision, but he did not lose his good humour. When his wife Clementine suggested that the result might well be a blessing in disguise, he observed wryly, '*At the moment it seems quite effectively disguised.*'

Victorious Labour politicians who defeated Churchill's Conservatives in 1945. After the war, people voted for a new government in the hope that the war's end would bring a change for the better to everyone.

Lend-Lease Act of March 1941 (enabling Britain to borrow $10 billion of US aid by 1945) and a joint declaration of peace aims, known as the Atlantic Charter (August 1941).

In the end Churchill's success in forging an alliance between the USA, the USSR and Britain undermined his international position. In 1943 he had persuaded the Americans to participate in a Mediterranean campaign which led to invasion of Sicily and Italy, and he was influential at the conference in Tehran between the USSR, USA and Britain (November-December 1943) held to discuss conduct of the war and the arrangement of the post-war world. But by 1944, as the might of Soviet and US forces began to make itself felt, Britain had become the third and least powerful member of the Allied coalition. Despite Churchill's presence at the Yalta Conference of February 1945, it was clear that, in future, power would lie with the USA and USSR superpowers. Churchill attended the Potsdam Conference of July 1945, but had to leave after his government lost the British general election.

With the Labour victory in 1945, Churchill became leader of the opposition. His speech at Fulton, Missouri, on 5 March 1946, in which he declared that, '*an iron curtain has descended across the Continent of Europe*', can be said to mark the start of bad relations between the USA and USSR. Churchill was prime minister again from 1951-1955.

Joseph Stalin (1879–1953)

When war broke out in Europe in September 1939, Stalin, secretary of the Soviet Communist Party, had been the supreme authority in the USSR for about ten years. During this period his ruthless rule had both helped and hindered the USSR prepare for the Second World War.

Based on government production targets set in three Five-Year Plans (1928-32, 1933-37 and 1938-42), Soviet industry made enormous advances. Steel production rose from 4 to 18.3 million tonnes, coal from 31 to 165.9 million tonnes, and oil from 11.7 to 31.1 million tonnes. Many of the new factories were sited in the east of the country, away from the vulnerable western border. By the time of the Nazi attack in 1941, the USSR was a major world industrial power, capable of producing enough tanks, aircraft and other weapons to wage war successfully against the Germans.

There was another, far less attractive side to Stalin's government. His fear of all opposition led Stalin to frequent 'purges' of the Communist Party, the armed forces, government officials and other potentially troublesome groups. Purges involved political commissars and the secret police spying on all officers and soldiers, and eliminating anyone else even vaguely associated with anti-Stalinist views.

Stalin became aware of the threat posed by Nazi Germany before any Western leader. But because he was a totalitarian communist, whose regime was hated and feared by men such as Chamberlain, Stalin was

Stalin's Red Army in 1941
Although massive, at the outbreak of war the Red (Soviet) Army had serious weaknesses.
1 10,000 officers had been purged, leaving the army seriously short of experienced commanders.
2 Stalin, who at this stage had little military understanding, interfered in every aspect of his forces' operations.
3 The soldiers were poorly trained and much equipment was either lacking (eg radios) or largely out of date (eg tanks).

The Nazi-Soviet Pact, August 1939

Background Alarmed by the anti-Russian statements in *Mein Kampf* and the rapid German rearmament under Hitler, Stalin feared that, in time, the Nazis would try to expand German territory into the USSR. • Poland and the Western democracies refused to commit themselves to an alliance with the USSR. • In 1939 the USSR's industry and armed forces were not ready for war with so powerful a country as Germany.

The Pact Negotiated by foreign ministers Ribbentrop (Germany) and Molotov (USSR), the pact said:
• Neither country would attack the other or support the other's enemies. • (Secret clause) Eastern Europe would be divided between Nazi and Soviet spheres of influence.

Results • Hitler was free to invade Poland. • Stalin bought time to prepare for a possible war with Germany. • There was a chance, Stalin believed, that the nations of Western Europe would fight each other to a standstill, leaving the USSR the dominant power on the continent.

unable to persuade them to take his warnings seriously. During the 1930s there were three dominant types of government in Europe: democracy, fascism and communism. They were all suspicious of each other, but before 1939 most democratic leaders feared communism more than fascism.

Isolated from other European states, Stalin went his own way. He made treaties with neighbouring countries, such as the Baltic states and Czechoslovakia. On a more practical level, he sent military assistance to the Chinese fighting the Japanese and to the Republicans in the Spanish Civil War. After the Czechoslovakian crisis of 1938 Stalin was desperate to stall the coming German attack, and agreed to the Nazi-Soviet Non-Aggression Pact of 23 August 1939.

Stalin's role during the war is not easy to judge. He insisted on overseeing every aspect of the Soviet forces. He undermined the army's morale with political arrests and executions, and was certainly not a great commander. But he gradually learned to trust and support men more skilled than himself, such as Red

A Soviet purge committee at work, 1933. The purges of people suspected of opposing Stalin deprived the USSR of many of its most able citizens.

Army Commander Zhukov, and they brought the USSR the victories it needed. His drive helped the modernization and re-equipment of Soviet forces, although they never matched the Germans for efficiency. At crucial moments, as in June 1941 and the assault on Moscow at the end of the year, he lost control of events. Overall, however, he provided the Soviet people with a focus for their dogged resistance.

Stalin was suspicious of his British and US allies because he knew they disliked communism. He was particularly annoyed that they did not invade Western Europe before 1944. At one stage he even tried to persuade them to open up a 'second front' by hinting that he might come to a separate agreement with Hitler. At the Tehran, Yalta and Potsdam Conferences Stalin proved a tough negotiator. His great fear was that after the defeat of fascism the Western Allies would turn their might against an isolated and exhausted USSR.

Both during and after the war Stalin did all he could to ensure that never again would his country be invaded from the west. He had taken the first steps even before the defeat of Germany, often refusing to support non-communist resistance movements. By 1949, communist governments, backed by Soviet

Russian soldiers taken prisoner by the German armies that invaded Russia in June 1941. Stalin was so shocked by the speed and success of the German invasion that he remained in drunken isolation for days. He reappeared full of determination and energy.

troops, were set up in the countries occupied by the Red Army – East Germany, Poland, Czechoslovakia, Hungary, Romania, Albania and Bulgaria. In 1949 COMECON was formed to bind these countries together economically. (Although communist, former Yugoslavia never came wholly under Soviet influence.) Many Western observers said that the establishment of a Soviet bloc in Eastern Europe was an example of Stalin's aggression. It can be argued that the Soviet leader's behaviour was defensive, that he was only trying to defend his regime against threats from the democracies. The USA was far wealthier than the USSR and after 1947 it poured economic aid into Europe to support friendly governments. Moreover, the USA had the atomic bomb, a weapon not possessed by the USSR until 1949. Was the West as much to blame as Stalin for the mistrust which led to the era of conflict between the two superpowers?

A 1938 French cartoon showing what the democratic West thought of Stalin's totalitarian regime – the placard reads, 'We are truly happy'. The figure on the left is a Russian worker; the man holding a gun on him is Stalin. Three years later Stalin had become the West's most powerful ally. Soon after the end of the Second World War, the West and the USSR were in conflict again.

Hirohito (1901–1989)

From 1926 to 1945 Japan was theoretically ruled by Emperor Hirohito. In fact he was really only a symbol. Real power rested with industrial combines and the party of the extreme nationalists (the *Toseiha*), who had close links with the army.

Hirohito's position was a strange one. As emperor he was regarded by most Japanese as a divine figure, whose word could not be challenged. All laws and commands went out in his name. He attended cabinet meetings, although he generally kept quiet because he was supposed to be above politics. Army officers were pledged to absolute obedience to the emperor. One reason why they fought on for so long against hopeless odds in 1945 was that they did not wish to disgrace their emperor or reduce his status. Yet Hirohito had never been keen on the war, and on 15 August 1945 he broke with tradition by using a radio broadcast to order his people to surrender.

The Japanese army, dominated by the *Toseiha*, became heavily

The Japanese army and politics

The political importance of the Japanese army was based on • A strong traditional respect for the military. • The independence of all military matters from civilian control. • Powerful reserve organizations. • Compulsory civilian military training (1925). • The 1936 law which said that only a serving officer could be war minister. • The influence on civilian matters of the Imperial Headquarters, which was controlled by the army.

Emperor Hirohito on horseback. In theory, Hirohito was Japan's ruler.

involved in politics in the 1920s. By the 1930s, as the political scene became more chaotic, the army had emerged as a stable and united force capable of directing policy. That policy included aggression towards neighbouring states, and in 1931 Japan took over the Chinese province of Manchuria. Three years later it formed the Anti-Comintern (anti-communist) Pact with Nazi Germany. Full-scale war with China followed in 1937, and the plan for a Greater East Asia Co-Prosperity Sphere in 1938. Believing it was not his job to get involved in such decisions, Hirohito did not interfere.

A far more influential figure was General Tojo, the leading member of the Japanese militarist party. Having served in the army, Tojo became deputy war minister in 1938, war minister in 1940 and prime minister on 14 October 1941. From then until his resignation in July 1944 it was he, not the emperor, who dominated the Japanese government. Convinced that war with the USA was inevitable, he authorized the Pearl Harbor attack. Tojo then reorganized the

General Tojo, the most influential member of the Japanese wartime government. He failed in his attempt to commit suicide in 1945 and was executed by the Allies as a war criminal.

All that remained of the city of Hiroshima after an atomic bomb had been detonated above it. This awful destruction persuaded Hirohito that Japan would have to surrender.

Japanese administration controlling the country's new empire and appointed himself chief of staff in February 1944. After the war he was found guilty of war crimes and hanged, along with six other Japanese leaders.

Hirohito, the man for whom Tojo and his forces were supposed to be fighting, remained in the background, keeping his views to himself. He emerged only at the very end of the war. In 1945 he requested Tojo to seek a negotiated peace with the Americans before Japan was crushed. Finally convinced by the dropping of an atomic bomb on Hiroshima that surrender was the only course left open to his people, Hirohito formally submitted to the USA.

Following the Japanese surrender the Allies were not quite sure what to do with Hirohito. The Chinese, Australians and New Zealanders wanted him put on trial for war crimes. The Americans decided against this, believing that the emperor would be a valuable right-wing force for stability in post-war Japan. So after he had admitted he was not a god, he was allowed to keep his title.

Hirohito remained a controversial figure for the rest of his life. Many Allied war veterans thought it was a disgrace that he was allowed to make a state visit to Britain in 1971. They said that although the emperor might not have been personally responsible for Japanese acts of aggression and apparent barbarity, he had the power to stop them but did not use it. The emperor's supporters argued that he had never been a political figure and could not be held responsible for what had been done in his name. Do you think people can be blamed for not doing what others think they should have done?

Emperor Hirohito on a visit to London. As the Japanese head of state, Hirohito visited Europe in 1971. Although the visit was criticized by some Allied war veterans, it helped re-establish good relations between Britain and Japan.

Chiang Kai-shek (1887–1975)

Chiang Kai-shek was president of China through-out the era of the Second World War. But his country was divided between the Communists and Chiang's Nationalists, and partly occupied by the Japanese. As a result the president never had the sort of influence one might expect of the leader of the country with the largest population in the world.

Following the overthrow of the imperial government in the revolution of 1911, China entered a long period of domestic strife. After the death of the revolutionary leader Sun Yat-sen in 1925, General Chiang rapidly built up his power. By 1928 he was the most powerful man in the country. He was president, commander-in-chief of the army and chairman of the ruling *Kuomindang* (Nationalist) party.

Chiang's presidency was troubled from the beginning. The deeply corrupt *Kuomindang* was never very popular with the peasant classes, who made up most of the population. Party members diverted government funds into their own pockets, showed no real interest in democracy and made little effort to improve people's lives. The army was unreliable too, rebelling in 1930, 1933 and 1936.

From 1931, when the Japanese occupied the province of Manchuria, Chiang also had to contend with invaders. To make matters worse, he was never able to come to a lasting peace with the Chinese Communists. In 1931 the Communists established a Chinese Soviet Republic in Kiangsi province and there was a civil war until 1936.

Open war with Japan in 1937 brought the Chinese Nationalists and Communists into temporary alliance. Their efforts were not enough to stop the Japanese advance, and by the end of 1938 the invaders held the whole of China's eastern coastline. Chiang was forced to move his headquarters further inland.

The outbreak of the Second World War brought Chiang new hope. He joined officially with the Allies on 9 December 1941. After Pearl Harbor he received plentiful American aid and in 1943 he was regarded as important enough to meet Roosevelt and Churchill at the Cairo Conference. During the previous year US

Chiang Kai-shek (left) meeting President Roosevelt and Prime Minister Churchill on equal terms, in Cairo in 1943. Although Chiang was theoretically head of one of the mightiest nations on earth, the Allies found him a disappointing ally.

Chiang Kai-shek at the age of 87, shortly before his death. Although ruler of the island of Taiwan, he insisted to the end that he was in fact President of the whole of China.

Lieutenant-General Stilwell had been sent to China to advise Chiang in his struggle against the Japanese. Chiang and Stilwell (who soon recognized the president's military incompetence and offended him with the nickname Peanut) did not get on. The American was called home in 1944. In 1945 Chiang's forces regained some territory from the Japanese, but by then the war was almost over.

With the withdrawal of Japanese troops from China, almost at once the Communists and Nationalists resumed their old hostilities. For a while the USA backed Chiang and tried to mediate between him and the Communist leaders Mao Tse-tung and Chou En-li. But after January 1947 they left Chiang to fend for himself.

The end for Chiang was not long coming. The Communists received widespread popular support and rapidly drove the Nationalists back to the sea. Peking fell in January 1949 and later that year Chiang fled to the island of Formosa (Taiwan). He stayed there for the remaining twenty-five years of his life, dreaming in vain of one day returning to the country of which he still believed himself to be president.

Chiang's career may suggest that individuals influence the course of events only when they are in tune with forces more powerful than themselves. Would this help to explain why Mao succeeded where Chiang failed?

Mao Tse-tung
Mao was Chiang's most determined opponent. In 1934-5 he and other leaders saved the Communist army from the Nationalists by leading it on the famous 13,000-kilometre Long March to the northern Shensi province. He put the experience he gained fighting the Japanese in alliance with the Nationalists (1937-1945) to good effect in the ensuing civil war. In 1949 he became Chairman of the People's Republic of China. Unlike Chiang, Mao recognized the peasantry as the key to power in China, and in response to his promises of land and justice they flocked to him.

Franklin D Roosevelt (1882–1945)

'This', said Nazi leader Goebbels when he heard of the death of President Roosevelt in 12 April 1945, *'is the turning point'*. Of course Goebbels was wrong. Roosevelt was replaced as president by Harry S Truman and the USA fought on. But Goebbels and many of his contemporaries believed that Roosevelt was personally responsible for the way his country conducted the war.

Roosevelt was first elected president of the USA in November 1932, taking up office the following year. He offered the American people a New Deal to lift them out of economic depression, and during the early years of his presidency much of his time was taken up with domestic matters. His policies seemed to work and he was re-elected in 1936.

Pearl Harbor

The surprise Japanese air attack on the US Pacific naval base at Pearl Harbor on 7 December 1941 (*'a date that will live in infamy'* – Roosevelt) destroyed 19 US vessels and 120 aircraft, and killed 2,400 people. Congress declared war on Japan the next day. Critics of Roosevelt's administration have argued that his staff should have seen the attack coming and done more to defend against it. It has also been argued that some members of the government secretly wanted a show of Japanese aggression against the USA as a way of persuading the American people to back US entry into the war.

Roosevelt being sworn in as President of the USA in 1941 for an unequalled third term of office. To win the previous year's election, he had played down his willingness for the USA to join the Second World War.

In 1940, when Roosevelt was elected to a third term as president, he had told his people what they wanted to hear: *'your boys will not be sent to any foreign wars.'* But in 1939 he had stated that, *'When peace has been broken anywhere, the peace of all countries everywhere is in danger'*, and he did not really believe that the USA could stand and watch as Germany won control of the Atlantic and Japan the Pacific. His attitude was based on two viewpoints: the USA had a moral duty to uphold democracy, and the country would be endangered if much of the rest of the world fell into the hands of dictators. Thus, while remaining officially neutral, he encouraged the build-up of the US fleet and did what he could to assist Britain and to contain the Japanese. He swapped fifty old US destroyers for the use of British naval bases in the Caribbean and the Atlantic, stepped up aid through the Lend-Lease Act of March 1941 and allowed the US Navy to escort convoys most of the way across the Atlantic. In July 1941, alarmed at Japan's aggression in the Far East (particularly in China) and its fascist links, he froze all Japanese funds in the USA and later insisted that talks with the Japanese would have to be conducted on his own terms. Diplomatic negotiations were in progress when news of the Japanese attack on Pearl Harbor came through.

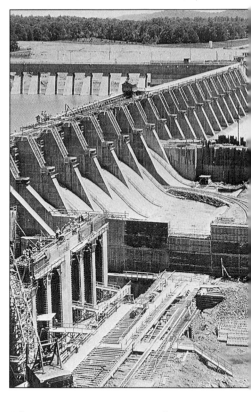

The Watts Bar Dam on the Tennessee River, built in 1937 as part of President Roosevelt's federal economic recovery package, known as the New Deal.

The President's Powers
American government operates within a written Constitution, first drawn up in 1787. Two key principles underlie central administration: the separation of powers and checks and balances. In theory these mean that policy is the responsibility of the president and lawmaking the job of Congress. The two institutions are quite separate and have ways of limiting each other's powers. (eg Congress makes laws, but they have to be signed by the president to become valid.) One result of this is that the president's power in foreign affairs is much greater than in domestic issues. Although Congress declares war, the president is commander-in-chief of the forces, appoints all ambassadors and controls US foreign policy.

Britain and her allies found American unwillingness to enter the struggle against fascism hard to understand. They failed to recognize that US politicians saw themselves as part of the New World, whose people rejected the squabbles of the Old World as having nothing directly to do with them. The famous aviator Charles Lindbergh expressed this view most forcibly when he said in April 1941, *'we in this country have a right to think of the welfare of America first . . . If we concentrate on our defences and build up the strength that this nation should maintain, no foreign army will ever attempt to land on American shores.'* Only the sneak attack on Pearl Harbor and Hitler's declaration of war four days later convinced American neutrals that it was now impossible for their country to stay out of the war.

Roosevelt giving Churchill's famous 'V-for-Victory' sign. After Pearl Harbor the friendship between the two men probably gave Britain more influence in world affairs than it had had before.

Those who support Roosevelt's management of US affairs during the war praise three things. Firstly, the efficient way in which he used his country's industrial might to create a gigantic war machine capable of upholding its allies and grinding down its enemies. Secondly, his demand, often against the wishes of the military, that co-operation between the Allies was more important than doing what was immediately best for the USA. And thirdly, his insistence that the war was a crusade for, *'four essential freedoms: freedom of speech and expression . . . freedom of every person to worship God in his own way . . . freedom from want . . . [and] freedom from fear.'*

Roosevelt's love of freedom and justice made him a champion of the idea of a United Nations Organization to oversee the post-war world. In August 1941, while the USA was still at peace, he joined with Churchill in producing the Atlantic Charter, outlining eight *'global principles'* for international understanding and

co-operation. These were adopted by twenty-six countries who signed the United Nations Declaration at the president's official residence, the White House, on 1 January 1942. The United Nations itself was formally set up thirteen days after Roosevelt's death, and came into effect in October. In some ways it is his most enduring monument.

Throughout his long presidency Roosevelt had plenty of critics. They believed that he did not have a clear or realistic grasp of the overall world picture. He was too trusting of Stalin, they said, and overestimated the power of Chiang Kai-shek's Nationalists. (After 1945 the USSR seized Eastern Europe and Chiang was driven from China.) The president's opponents in Congress and the armed forces accused him of prolonging the war by insisting on unconditional surrender of the Axis powers, and by backing plans to invade northern Europe over the Channel rather than push north from the Mediterranean.

Nevertheless Roosevelt inspired deep respect and love. When he died of a sudden stroke less than a month before Germany's surrender, American troops at the battlefront wept openly. (Described in Hugh Brogan's, *History of the United States of America.*)

Roosevelt and Churchill, who were great friends, at a press conference in Casablanca, January 1943.

Roosevelt and Stalin

Roosevelt, the elected leader of the world's largest democracy, and Stalin, the communist dictator, made strange allies. For a long time Roosevelt believed that the USSR's suspicious attitude was partly the result of the way the Western democracies had treated the country before 1941. He had recognized the USSR in 1933 and during the war sought to break down Stalin's reserve by treating him as a trusted friend. This did not make Stalin any easier to deal with. Perhaps Roosevelt was too much of an idealist, or perhaps he was right when he confessed, 'I don't know a good Russian from a bad Russian . . . I don't understand the Russians.'

Harry S Truman (1884–1972)

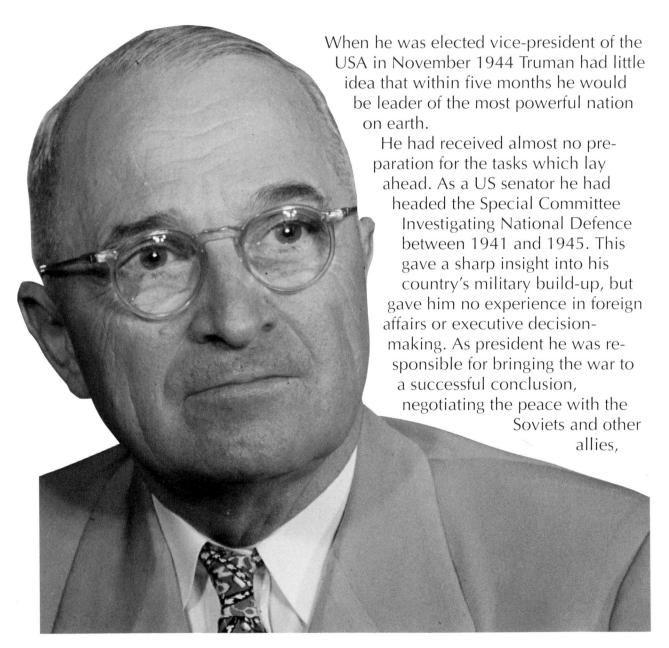

When he was elected vice-president of the USA in November 1944 Truman had little idea that within five months he would be leader of the most powerful nation on earth.

He had received almost no preparation for the tasks which lay ahead. As a US senator he had headed the Special Committee Investigating National Defence between 1941 and 1945. This gave a sharp insight into his country's military build-up, but gave him no experience in foreign affairs or executive decision-making. As president he was responsible for bringing the war to a successful conclusion, negotiating the peace with the Soviets and other allies,

The Truman Doctrine
Truman set out his new foreign policy in a speech to Congress on 12 March 1947:
'I believe that it must be the policy of the United States to support free peoples who are resisting attempted subjugation by armed minorities or by outside pressures. I believe we must assist free peoples to work out their own destinies in their own way.'

A German poster advertising the Marshall Plan, an offshoot of the Truman Doctrine. Under the terms of the Plan the USA gave the states of Western Europe $17 billion to speed their recovery from the war.

helping to set up the United Nations, and deciding whether or not to use the atomic bomb. To many people's surprise, Truman adapted to his new job very easily.

Truman delayed the start of the Allied Potsdam Conference (17 July, 1945) until after the successful testing of an atomic bomb. He hoped it would give him an extra bargaining counter in his discussions with Stalin. As it turned out, since they were not prepared to fight their old ally, the Americans could do little about the presence of Soviet troops in most of Eastern Europe. Nevertheless, the Potsdam discussions seemed amicable enough and there were not many obvious signs of the future rift between the two superpowers.

The decision to use the atomic bomb to bring the war against Japan to a swift end was entirely Truman's.

Many scientists said that the weapon was too terrible to be used. Military advisers, on the other hand, urged that unless the weapon was used the war would drag on for months, resulting in terrible loss of American life. The president was convinced by their arguments, and atomic explosions destroyed the cities and residents of Hiroshima (6 August) and Nagasaki (9 August). Japan surrendered five days later. Did Truman make the right decision?

By the end of 1946 Truman was sure that it had not been enough for the USA to win the war – they had to win the peace as well. By that he meant resisting the expansion of communism, *'primarily through economic and financial aid'*. The Truman Doctrine meant that for the first time the USA would become actively involved as a global power in peacetime. It was, as he said, *'a turning point in American foreign policy.'*

Although Truman said that he wished to support 'free peoples', it can be argued that what he was doing was building up a network of states friendly to the USA. In other words, his policy was as much about defending US interests as those of the countries he assisted. That is certainly how the Soviets saw it.

The inside of what had been a school in Nagasaki. Most of the children and teachers would have been killed by the atomic bomb dropped on the city in 1945. The decision to use this terrible weapon was made by Harry S Truman, then US president.

Great men?

This book began with two questions. How different were the wartime powers wielded by the leaders of democratic states from those of the dictators? Did these war leaders really exercise as much influence as people have thought they did?

At the Tehran Conference of 1943 Stalin, Roosevelt and Churchill met for dinner. During the meal the American adviser Harry L Hopkins said light-heartedly that, *'the provisions of the British Constitution and the powers of the War Cabinet are just whatever Winston Churchill wants them to be.'* The prime minister rejected the comment, saying that, *'I was the only one of our trinity* [Stalin, Roosevelt and himself] *who could at any moment be dismissed from power.'* He went on, *'The President's term of office was fixed, and his powers not only as President but as Commander-in-Chief were almost absolute . . .* [and] *Stalin appeared to be, and at this moment certainly was, all-powerful in Russia.'*

Firefighters tackling a blaze after a bombing raid. Decisions made by wartime leaders affected the lives of millions and millions of people. Many of them died during the war, whether they came from democracies or dictatorships, through no choice of their own.

German troops moving into Holland, May 1940. It is inconceivable that any Dutch leader, however brilliant, could have saved the country from invasion.

It was actually very unlikely that Churchill would be fired. He had never been elected prime minister by the British people, and until an election was held Churchill was never really in danger of losing power (he did lose the election of 1945). The war had brought special circumstances in which all leaders were granted far more power than they would have had in peacetime. No leader lost power until the war was ending; Mussolini, Hitler and Tojo died because their countries lost the war, and Churchill lost an election held after peace had been declared in Europe. It could be said that none of the leaders was very different in the power they held until the war was ending. So the answer to the first question is perhaps that the authority of the various national leaders was not all that different. Whatever the form of government in peacetime, in wartime the leader was allowed massive powers to conduct affairs effectively.

This brings us to our second question. Did the individual leaders really matter? Obviously, to some extent they did. When the advice of the generals and politicians had been taken, strategic decisions, such as that to drop the atomic bomb, had to be taken personally. Some would argue, however, that they should be seen only within a wider framework. For example, The British could only expect to resist an invasion in 1940 because they lived on an island and so had a reasonable chance of surviving. Nothing could have saved the Dutch from the German tanks in May 1940. Similarly Hitler's leadership might have directed the German people to incredible feats of arms in 1939-41. But without Germany's desire to overcome the bitter humiliations of 1918-26 and the backing of one of the most powerful economies in the world, his calls for a 'Thousand-Year Reich' would have been so much hot air.

In history, individuals and greater forces are woven together in a tangle which we cannot ever hope to unravel completely. Therefore before we hasten to praise or blame the so-called 'great leaders', it is worth bearing in mind the age-old saying: *'Cometh the hour, cometh the man.'* You cannot have one without the other.

Opinion is divided about the extent to which the Second World War was influenced by 'great men'. This British propaganda poster of 1940 suggests that events would be decided not by individuals, but by the whole nation working together.

Glossary

Absolute   Having complete power.

Allies   The USA, Britain and the other countries fighting the Axis powers.

Anschluss   Union, particularly that of Germany and Austria in 1938.

Anti-Commintern Pact   The agreement to resist the spread of communism made by Germany, Japan and Italy in the 1930s.

Anti-semitism   Hostility towards the Jewish people.

Armistice   A signed cease-fire.

Axis   The alliance of Germany, Italy and Japan in the 1930s.

Blitzkrieg   Lightning War: the strategy of striking at the enemy hard and fast, using aircraft and armour.

Cabinet   The small group of leading government ministers.

Charismatic   Having a personality attractive to others.

Civil war   A war fought between people of a single country.

Coalition   A group formed by more than one party or country.

Communism   A political theory believing that all people should be equal and there should be no private ownership of such things as factories and farms.

Concentration camp   A prison camp for specific groups of people – for example Jews or homosexuals. In Nazi Germany many people were killed in such camps.

Constitutional monarchy   A form of government in which the monarch is head of state but has no political power.

Convoy   A number of ships sailing together.

D-Day   The code name for the Allied landings on the Normandy beaches, 6 June 1944.

Demilitarized zone   Territory where no troops or fortifications are permitted.

Democracy   Government by elected representatives of the people.

Depression   A severe economic slump. Depressions often involve high unemployment.

Dictatorship   Government by a single figure, the dictator.

Division   A large self-sufficient army unit.

Fascism   A totalitarian political system laying stress on nationalism and the figure of the leader.

Final Solution   The Nazi decision to exterminate all the Jewish people living within German-held territory.

Foreign policy   A country's policy towards other states.

Intelligence   The information a state's information-gathering service collects.

League of Nations   The unsuccessful international organization set up after the First World War to preserve peace and develop co-operation between the countries of the world.

Left wing   Inclined towards socialism or communism.

Liberal   The political belief which stresses the rights and freedoms of the individual.

Maginot Line   A defensive line built 1929-34 in eastern France to defend against a possible German attack. In 1940 the Germans went round it by advancing through Belgium.

Mobilize   Prepare for war.

NATO   (The North Atlantic Treaty Organization) An anti-communist defensive alliance set up in 1949 by the USA and its European allies.

Neutral   Not taking sides.

New Deal   President Roosevelt's package of measures, introduced in the USA during the 1930s, intended to boost the US economy. It involved the federal (national) government more closely in local affairs.

Occupy   Take over another territory, which is thereby occupied.

Offensive   A broad-ranging attack.

Purge   Get rid of supposedly unwanted or dangerous individuals.

Re-armament   Building up armed forces after a period of peace.

Reparations   Payments to meet the cost of the war made by those who have been defeated.

Repression   Driving out all opposition.

Republic   A state not governed by a monarch.

Sanctions   Measures taken against a state, but not involving war.

Socialism   A political theory which believes that all powerful organizations (businesses etc) should be in the hands of the state.

Totalitarianism   A political system which places all power directly in the hands of the state and its leader(s).

USSR   The Union of Soviet Socialist Republics – the communist state which replaces the Russian Empire after the 1917 revolution.

Versailles, Treaty of   The treaty imposed on Germany after the First World War.

Vichy France   The part of France which submitted to the Germans in 1940 and was allowed a measure of self-government. It was occupied by the Germans in 1942.

Books to read

Churchill and the Second World War Stewart Ross (Wayland, 1987)

Hitler and the Third Reich Bradley (Franklin Watts, 1990)

Italy under Mussolini Leeds (Wayland, 1988)

Origins of the Second World War Peter Allen (Wayland, 1991)

Rise of Fascism Peter Chrisp (Wayland, 1991)

Roosevelt and the Americans at War Cross (Franklin Watts, 1990)

USSR Under Stalin Stewart Ross (Wayland, 1991)

Timeline

1918	11 November	Armistice ends First World War.
1919	28 June	Treaty of Versailles signed.
1921	29 July	Hitler chairman of Nazi party.
1924		Hitler writes *Mein Kampf*.
1928		Stalin dominant in USSR.
1929	29 October	Wall Street Crash begins world economic depression.
1931		Japan takes over Chinese province of Manchuria.
	14 April	Spain becomes a republic.
1932	7 January	Germany stops paying war reparations.
1933	30 January	Hitler appointed chancellor of Germany.
	23 March	German Enabling Law.
	14 July	Nazis become the only legal party in Germany.
	2 August	Hitler made Führer.
1934	October	Civil violence in Spain.
1935	15 March	Germany openly rearming.
	2 October	Italian troops invade Ethiopia.
	19 October	Ineffective League of Nations sanctions on Italy.
1936	February	Left wins elections in Spain; civil violence.
	3 March	Britain increases defence expenditure.
	8 March	German troops enter Rhineland.
	18 July	Spanish Civil War begins.
	1 October	Franco head of state in Spain.
	1 November	Rome-Berlin Axis.
	18 November	Franco government recognized by Hitler and Mussolini.
1937	27 April	German aircraft destroy Guernica during Spanish Civil War.
	7 July	Japan attacks China.
	6 November	Italy joins Germany and Japan in Anti-Comintern Pact.
1938		Stalin's enemies being purged in USSR.
	4 February	Hitler becomes commander of all German armed forces.
	12 March	*Anschluss* (union) of Germany and Austria begins.
	12 August	German troops mobilize over Czechoslovakian crisis.
	27 September	Royal Navy mobilized.
	30 September	Czechoslovakian crisis defused at Munich Conference.
	October	Chiang Kai-shek's government moves to Chungking.
	1 October	German troops into Sudetenland.
1939	26 January	Franco's forces capture Barcelona.
	27 February	Britain and France recognize Franco's government.
	15 March	Czechoslovakia occupied.
	28 March	Franco's forces enter Madrid.
	31 March	Britain and France promise to uphold Polish independence.
	18 April	USSR suggests alliance with Britain and France.
	28 April	Hitler rejects peace proposals from President Roosevelt.
	2 May	Hitler and Mussolini's 'Pact of Steel'.
	23 August	Nazi-Soviet Non-Aggression Pact.
	1 September	Germany invades Poland.
	3 September	Britain and France declare war on Germany.
	17 September	Soviet troops into Poland.
	6 October	Hitler rejects peace moves by Britain and France.
	30 November	USSR invades Finland.

1940	7 April	Germans attack Norway and Denmark.
	10 May	German attack on Holland, France and Belgium.
		Churchill replaces Chamberlain as prime minister.
	29 May	Beginning of Dunkirk evacuation.
	June	Soviet troops invade Baltic states.
		Battle of Britain begins (ends September).
	10 June	Mussolini declares war on Britain and France.
	22 June	France surrenders.
	14 September	Italy invades Egypt.
	27 September	Japan, Germany and Italy form Tripartite Pact.
	28 October	Italy invades Greece.
	5 November	Roosevelt re-elected president of USA.
1941	9 February	German troops to North Africa.
	11 March	Lend-Lease Act signed.
	22 June	German invasion of the USSR.
	July	Embargoes on sale of oil and steel to Japan.
	7 August	Stalin supreme commander of Soviet forces.
	17 October	General Tojo prime minister of Japan.
	November	German forces halted outside Moscow.
	7 December	Japanese attack on Pearl Harbor.
	8 December	USA and Britain declare war on Japan.
	9 December	China declares war on Japan and Germany.
	11 December	Germany and Italy declare war on USA.
1942	20 January	Wannsee Conference proposes 'Final Solution'.
	15 February	Singapore falls to Japanese.
	6 May	Battle of Coral Sea (ends 8 May).
	4 June	Battle of Midway.
	July	Battle of Stalingrad begins (ends February 1943).
	23 October	Battle of El Alamein (ends 4 November).
	11 November	Germans move into Vichy France.

1943	5 July	Beginning of Battle of Kursk (ends 23 August).
	10 July	Allies land in Sicily.
	26 July	Mussolini resigns.
	3 September	Allies land in Italy.
	13 October	Italy declares war on Germany.
	28 November	Tehran Conference opens.
1944	March	Soviet troops into Poland.
	17 April	Fresh Japanese offensive in China.
	6 June	D-Day Allied landings in Normandy.
	23 June	Soviet offensive begins.
	18 July	General Tojo resigns as Japanese prime minister.
	21 August	Dumbarton Oaks Conference sets out framework for United Nations.
	6 October	Soviets into Czechoslovakia and Hungary.
	20 October	US forces land in Philippines.
	November	Unrelenting bombing of Japan begins.
	16 December	Unsuccessful German offensive in Ardennes begins.
1945	4 February	Yalta Conference opens.
	1 April	US forces land on Okinawa.
	12 April	Roosevelt dies – Truman becomes president of USA.
	20 April	Russians reach Berlin.
	7 May	Germany surrenders.
	26 June	United Nations formed.
	17 July	Potsdam Conference opens.
	6 August	Atomic bomb dropped on Hiroshima.
	8 August	USSR declares war on Japan.
	9 August	Atomic bomb dropped on Nagasaki.
	14 August	Japan surrenders.
	October	Civil war in China.
1946	5 March	Churchill's 'Iron Curtain' speech.
1947	12 March	Truman Doctrine outlined.
	5 June	Marshall Plan put forward.
1948	24 June	Soviets begin blockade of West Berlin (ends 12 May 1949).
1949	January	COMECON established.
	4 April	NATO formed.

Index